PEACHY'S BIG MOVE

Written by Georgia Carrol

Illustrated by Kristen Trauter

For all the little hearts heading to new places—

May this story remind you that no matter where you go, home is wherever you're together.

And to Peachy, who teaches us that love and warmth travel with us, from one cozy corner to the next.

The day began just like any other. The sun peeked over the horizon, the sky turned bright blue, and Peachy, the little calico, woke her humans right on time.
After all, a kitty's got to eat!

But today
wasn't just
any day.
Today was a
special day.

Today was
moving day!
Peachy just
didn't realize
yet.

As the humans prepared breakfast, Peachy tried to enjoy her meal, but something was off.

"Where is my favorite pink bowl? Where's my paw print placemat? Why can't I splish splash in my water fountain?" Peachy was confused, so she decided to go calm down and relax on her fluffy rug.

"Wait a second! Where's my fluffy rug?!"
Peachy started to worry. "I better check my toy bin, just to
make sure." But when she looked, her toys were gone too!
"Someone needs to tell me what's going on, right MEOW!"

meeeeeoooOOW

Peachy took a deep breath and stomped over to her humans. She let out a loud demanding answers. But her humans were too busy to notice her distress.

Peachy explored the house.
She peeked into every room and
discovered that all her belongings
were packed away in boxes.
Her bed, her toys, even her favorite
scratching post

—everything was missing!

"Why would they put everything in boxes?" Peachy worried. "Are they leaving me behind?"

Just then, the doorbell rang.

A team of movers arrived to load everything into a big truck. "This is my chance," Peachy thought. "I need to get to the bottom of what's going on!"

With a brave heart, Peachy followed the movers closely,
making sure they carefully loaded her special bowl,
fluffy rug, and toy bin.

Once the truck was loaded, Peachy jumped into the passenger seat, determined to keep an eye on her prized possessions.

The ride was bumpy and long, but Peachy stayed alert; after all, she had a job to do.

When they finally arrived, Peachy leapt into action. She supervised the movers, making sure every box labeled "Peachy" was handled with extra care.

Inside the new house, Peachy's humans began unpacking.

To her delight, her special bowl was placed in the new kitchen.

Her fluffy rug was spread out in the living room.

Her toy bin was set right by the ginormous bay window.

In all the commotion, Peachy didn't even realize that this new space was a beautiful, 3-bedroom, 3-bathroom detached home, with generous-sized living and dining rooms, with a retreat-like primary bedroom and gleaming hardwood floors throughout.

Feeling proud, Peachy strutted around her
new home, checking every corner.
Everything was perfect,
just as it should be.

She had done it! She had made sure the new house was ready with all their favourite items, not just for herself, but for her humans too.

As Peachy curled up with her humans, all calm and happy, she felt a sense of familiarity. She had faced a big, scary day, and she was triumphant. Peachy the brave little calico, had conquered moving day.

As the stars twinkled in the night sky, Peachy purred softly, knowing that no matter what happened, she and her humans would always be together.

SPECIAL THANKS

There is not one day that goes by that I do not feel the utmost gratitude for all of the amazing, supportive people I have in my life.

Lubby Doo, you are my rock and the reason that I feel so confident to make all of my "far fetched" ideas into a reality. It is the stability you provide that allows me to truly soar.

Kristen, thank you for taking my sweet peachy and turning her into the cutest character, while nailing the complete vision. You were ready not only to meet expectations but exceed them in tight timelines. I appreciate you never telling me no, or that something is out of reach.

Peachy, my inspiration to write this book. My sweet little murmy who is my angel, who came to me at just the right time. You bring unlimited joy to my life, and now it's time for you to bring joy to the world!

Georgia

XO

Author
Georgia Carrol

Georgia is a third-generation real estate professional and a passionate advocate for making transitions easier for families. Having grown up with a love for homes and a deep understanding of what makes a house a home, she understands that moving can be a big change, especially for little ones. Inspired by her own sweet kitty, Peachy, she wrote this story to help children find comfort in new places and to remind them that as long as we're together, we're always home. Georgia lives in Ottawa, Canada and loves spending time with her family and kitties.

Illustrator
Kristen Trauter

Kristen is an illustrator from Ottawa, Ontario with a background in animation, where she developed her expertise in character design and visual storytelling. Her experience has given her a unique skill set, enabling her to bring characters to life with vibrant, expressive details that captivate audiences of all ages.

Known for her playful yet thoughtful style, Kristen's work reflects her passion for creating imagery that connects emotionally. She believes in the power of visual storytelling to spark imagination and inspire young readers, bringing warmth and personality to every project she undertakes.

Meet Peachy

Peachy is an inquisitive calico cat with a knack for being in the know. Whether it's a creaking door or a whispered conversation, Peachy needs to be part of the action at all times. Her purr? It's not just content; it's a full-on rumble that fills the room. She's got a soft spot for her favorite treats and can't resist the crinkly charm of her beloved pom pom toy.

Every morning, Peachy insists on starting her day with a fresh dish of wet food before heading out to the balcony to watch over the neighborhood, as she is the queen of her little world. When she's not on duty, you'll find her stretched out in the warmest, sunniest spot she can find—because Peachy always knows where the sun is.

www.ingramcontent.com/pod-product-compliance
Lightning Source LLC
Chambersburg PA
CBHW041502120626
46547CB00003B/510